Hymns

VOLUME I

CARA COBBLE TRANTHAM

Study Suggestions

We believe that the Bible is true, trustworthy, and timeless and that it is vitally important for all believers. These study suggestions are intended to help you more effectively study Scripture as you seek to know and love God through His Word.

SUGGESTED STUDY TOOLS

A Bible

A double-spaced, printed copy of the Scripture passages that this study covers. You can use a website like *www.biblegateway.com* to copy the text of a passage and print out a double-spaced copy to be able to mark on easily

A journal to write notes or prayers

Pens, colored pencils, and highlighters

A dictionary to look up unfamiliar words

HOW TO USE THIS STUDY

Begin your study time in prayer. Ask God to reveal Himself to you, to help you understand what you are reading, and to transform you with His Word (Psalm 119:18).

Before you read what is written in each day of the study itself, read the assigned passages of Scripture for that day. Use your double-spaced copy to circle, underline, highlight, draw arrows, and mark in any way you would like to help you dig deeper as you work through a passage.

Read the daily written content provided for the current study day.

Answer the questions that appear at the end of each study day.

HOW TO STUDY THE BIBLE

The inductive method provides tools for deeper and more intentional Bible study.
To study the Bible inductively, work through the steps below after
reading background information on the book.

1 OBSERVATION & COMPREHENSION
Key question: What does the text say?

After reading the daily Scripture in its entirety at least once, begin working
with smaller portions of the Scripture. Read a passage of Scripture repetitively,
and then mark the following items in the text:

- Key or repeated words and ideas
- Key themes
- Transition words (Ex: therefore, but, because, if/then, likewise, etc.)
- Lists
- Comparisons and contrasts
- Commands
- Unfamiliar words (look these up in a dictionary)
- Questions you have about the text

2 INTERPRETATION
Key question: What does the text mean?

Once you have annotated the text, work through the following steps to
help you interpret its meaning:

- Read the passage in other versions for a better understanding of the text.
- Read cross-references to help interpret Scripture with Scripture.
- Paraphrase or summarize the passage to check for understanding.
- Identify how the text reflects the metanarrative of Scripture, which is the story of creation, fall, redemption, and restoration.
- Read trustworthy commentaries if you need further insight into the meaning of the passage.

3

APPLICATION
Key Question: How should the truth of this passage change me?

Bible study is not merely an intellectual pursuit. The truths about God, ourselves, and the gospel that we discover in Scripture should produce transformation in our hearts and lives. Answer the following questions as you consider what you have learned in your study:

- What attributes of God's character are revealed in the passage?

   Consider places where the text directly states the character of God, as well as how His character is revealed through His words and actions.

- What do I learn about myself in light of who God is?

   Consider how you fall short of God's character, how the text reveals your sin nature, and what it says about your new identity in Christ.

- How should this truth change me?

   A passage of Scripture may contain direct commands telling us what to do or warnings about sins to avoid in order to help us grow in holiness. Other times our application flows out of seeing ourselves in light of God's character. As we pray and reflect on how God is calling us to change in light of His Word, we should be asking questions like, "How should I pray for God to change my heart?" and "What practical steps can I take toward cultivating habits of holiness?"

THE ATTRIBUTES OF GOD

ETERNAL

God has no beginning
and no end. He always
was, always is,
and always will be.

HAB. 1:12 / REV. 1:8 / IS. 41:4

FAITHFUL

God is incapable of
anything but fidelity.
He is loyally devoted to
His plan and purpose.

2 TIM. 2:13 / DEUT. 7:9
HEB. 10:23

GOOD

God is pure; there is no
defilement in Him.
He is unable to sin, and
all He does is good.

GEN. 1:31 / PS. 34:8 / PS. 107:1

GRACIOUS

God is kind, giving
us gifts and benefits
we do not deserve.

2 KINGS 13:23 / PS. 145:8
IS. 30:18

HOLY

God is undefiled and
unable to be in the presence
of defilement. He is
sacred and set-apart.

REV. 4:8 / LEV. 19:2 / HAB. 1:13

INCOMPREHENSIBLE & TRANSCENDENT

God is high above and beyond
human understanding. He is
unable to be fully known.

PS. 145:3 / IS. 55:8-9
ROM. 11:33-36

IMMUTABLE

God does not change.
He is the same yesterday,
today, and tomorrow.

1 SAM. 15:29 / ROM. 11:29
JAMES 1:17

INFINITE

God is limitless. He exhibits
all of His attributes perfectly
and boundlessly.

ROM. 11:33-36 / IS. 40:28
PS. 147:5

JEALOUS

God is desirous of receiving
the praise and affection
He rightly deserves.

EX. 20:5 / DEUT. 4:23-24
JOSH. 24:19

JUST

God governs in
perfect justice. He acts in
accordance with justice.
In Him, there is no
wrongdoing or dishonesty.

IS. 61:8 / DEUT. 32:4 / PS. 146:7-9

LOVING

God is eternally, enduringly,
steadfastly loving and
affectionate. He does not
forsake or betray His
covenant love.

JN. 3:16 / EPH. 2:4-5 / 1 JN. 4:16

MERCIFUL

God is compassionate,
withholding from us the
wrath that we deserve.

TITUS 3:5 / PS. 25:10
LAM. 3:22-23

OMNIPOTENT

God is all-powerful;
His strength is unlimited.

MAT. 19:26 / JOB 42:1-2
JER. 32:27

OMNIPRESENT

God is everywhere;
His presencae is near
and permeating.

PROV. 15:3 / PS. 139:7-10
JER. 23:23-24

OMNISCIENT

God is all-knowing;
there is nothing
unknown to Him.

PS. 147:4 / I JN. 3:20
HEB. 4:13

PATIENT

God is long-suffering and
enduring. He gives ample
opportunity for people
to turn toward Him.

ROM. 2:4 / 2 PET. 3:9 / PS. 86:15

SELF-EXISTENT

God was not created
but exists by His
power alone.

PS. 90:1-2 / JN. 1:4 / JN. 5:26

SELF-SUFFICIENT

God has no needs and
depends on nothing, but
everything depends on God.

IS. 40:28-31 / ACTS 17:24-25
PHIL. 4:19

SOVEREIGN

God governs over all things;
He is in complete control.

COL. 1:17 / PS. 24:1-2
1 CHRON. 29:11-12

TRUTHFUL

God is our measurement
of what is fact. By Him
we are able to discern
true and false.

JN. 3:33 / ROM. 1:25 / JN. 14:6

WISE

God is infinitely
knowledgeable and is
judicious with His
knowledge.

IS. 46:9-10 / IS. 55:9 / PROV. 3:19

WRATHFUL

God stands in opposition to
all that is evil. He enacts
judgment according to
His holiness, righteousness,
and justice.

PS. 69:24 / JN. 3:36 / ROM. 1:18

Creation

In the beginning, God created the universe. He made the world and everything in it. He created humans in His own image to be His representatives on the earth.

Fall

The first humans, Adam and Eve, disobeyed God by eating from the fruit of the Tree of Knowledge of Good and Evil. Their disobedience impacted the whole world. The punishment for sin is death, and because of Adam's original sin, all humans are sinful and condemned to death.

Redemption

God sent His Son to become a human and redeem His people. Jesus Christ lived a sinless life but died on the cross to pay the penalty for sin. He resurrected from the dead and ascended into heaven. All who put their faith in Jesus are saved from death and freely receive the gift of eternal life.

Restoration

One day, Jesus Christ will return again and restore all that sin destroyed. He will usher in a new heaven and new earth where all who trust in Him will live eternally with glorified bodies in the presence of God.

Table of Contents

What a Friend We Have in Jesus

Joseph M. Scriven, ca. 1855

What a friend we have in Jesus,
All our sins and griefs to bear!
What a privilege to carry
Everything to God in prayer!
Oh, what peace we often forfeit,
Oh, what needless pain we bear,
All because we do not carry
Everything to God in prayer!

Have we trials and temptations?
Is there trouble anywhere?
We should never be discouraged—
Take it to the Lord in prayer.
Can we find a friend so faithful,
Who will all our sorrows share?
Jesus knows our every weakness;
Take it to the Lord in prayer.

Are we weak and heavy-laden,
Cumbered with a load of care?
Precious Savior, still our refuge—
Take it to the Lord in prayer.
Do thy friends despise, forsake thee?
Take it to the Lord in prayer!
In His arms He'll take and shield thee,
Thou wilt find a solace there.

Blessed Savior, Thou hast promised
Thou wilt all our burdens bear;
May we ever, Lord, be bringing
All to Thee in earnest prayer.
Soon in glory bright, unclouded,
There will be no need for prayer—
Rapture, praise, and endless worship
Will be our sweet portion there.

**week 1
day 1**

READ:

PSALM 25:14

JOHN 15:15

JAMES 2:23

What a Friend We Have in Jesus

Joseph Scriven was at the peak of his youth, enjoying his money, intelligence, a loving family, and a beautiful fiancé. The night before his wedding, his bride drowned in a tragic accident. Following this tragedy, Joseph relocated and made a new life for himself, one with a mission to help anyone in need. He became a friend to many, and he soon became known as the Good Samaritan of Cape Hope. One day, he got word that his mother was ill. He mailed her a letter, including a little poem that he had written to encourage her. Sometime later, a friend visited Joseph during his own time of illness. This friend noticed the poem that he had sent to his mother scribbled on a piece of paper on Joseph's bedside table. He asked Joseph who wrote the poem, and Joseph replied, "The Lord and I, between the two of us."

Psalm 25:14 says, "The secret counsel of the Lord is for those who fear him, and he reveals his covenant to them." Jesus is not a fair-weather friend. Nor is He a friend just for our tough times. He is a friend for every day. The Lord longs to commune with us. He longs to make known His covenant to us. He longs to call us friend. What "peace we often forfeit," and what "needless pain we bear," simply because we do not take Jesus, our friend, up on His offer of constant communication. Let us start today, taking everything before the Lord — the good and the bad. Let us not give up any more peace because we try to carry our burdens alone. Let us call on our true friend.

Questions

Meditate on Psalm 25:14. What does this verse teach you about friendship with the Lord?

Read Psalm 9:10. How does this verse grow your understanding of knowing the Lord's name? Why might this be important?

What are some ways that this hymn points your heart and mind to worshiping God?

Day by Day

Lina Sandell Berg, ca. 1865

Day by day and with each passing moment,
Strength I find to meet my trials here;
Trusting in my Father's wise bestowment,
I've no cause for worry or for fear.
He whose heard is kind beyond all measure
Gives unto each day what He deems best—
Lovingly, it's part of pain and pleasure,
Mingling toil with peace and rest.

Ev'ry day the Lord Himself is near me
With special mercy for each hour;
All my care He fain would bear, and cheer me,
He whose name is Counselor and Pow'r.
The protection of His child and treasure
Is a charge that on Himself He laid;
"As they days, they strength shall be in measure,"
This the pledge to me He made.

Help me then in every tribulation
So to trust They promises, O Lord,
That I lose not faith's sweet consolation
Offered me within Thy holy Word.
Help me, Lord, when toil and trouble meeting,
E'er to take, as from a father's hand,
One by one, the days, the moments fleeting,
Till I reach the promised land.

**week 1
day 2**

READ:

PSALM 46:1-3

EPHESIANS 2:7

PSALM 69:16

Day by Day

From a small child, Lina Sandell Berg was confined to her bed with paralysis. When she turned 16, she became miraculously healed from her condition and began writing hymns of praise to the Lord. When she was 26, she and her family were traveling by boat across a body of water when the boat lurched, and her father fell overboard and drowned before her very eyes. About ten years later, she married and contracted typhoid fever during her first pregnancy. Their only child died at birth, but she did not allow the hard things in her life to turn her eyes away from the Lord. Instead, she gave her broken heart to Jesus and fully trusted Him with her pain.

A broken heart would at times convince us that if God were truly good, He would not allow tragedies to occur. But as Lina learned, His heart is kind beyond all measure. Ephesians 2:7 says, "So that in the coming ages he might show the immeasurable riches of his grace through his kindness to us in Christ Jesus." Our definition of kindness does not begin to compare to the kindness and generosity of our Father. His "wise bestowment" leaves us without the need to worry for our future. We do not have to claw our way through life, grasping onto success, prosperity, and riches. When we trust that God has planned our day-by-day lives, we can rest in His provision. And when trials and tragedies come, we can know that we have never left His watchful eye. Knowing who God is gives us security when we do not understand. This beautiful song is rich in meaning and encourages us to take hold of the promise that our Father knows best.

Questions

Reflect on the words of Psalm 46:1-3. What does this passage teach you about God's character? How do the words of this hymn reflect this passage?

In what ways does Ephesians 2:7 give you hope in times of suffering? Why might this verse be important to remember when you experience difficulty?

Do you find it difficult to remember the Lord's nearness when you experience sorrow? How might remembering this song and the Scripture associated with it bring you peace?

Blest Be The Tie
That Binds

John Fawcett, ca. 1782

Blest be the tie that bind
our hearts in Christian love;
the fellowship of kindred minds
is like to that above.

Before our Father's throne
we pour our ardent prayers;
our fears, our hopes, our aims are one,
our comforts and our cares.

We share our mutual woes,
our mutual burdens bear,
and often for each other flows
the sympathizing tear.

When we are called to part,
it gives us inward pain;
but we shall still be joined in heart,
and hope to meet again.

This glorious hope revives
our courage by the way;
while each in expectation lives
and waits to see the day.

From sorrow, toil, and pain,
and sin, we shall be free;
and perfect love and friendship reign
through all eternity.

**week 1
day 3**

READ:
ROMANS 12:12-13
COLOSSIANS 3:16
MATTHEW 6:33

Blest Be the Tie that Binds

John Fawcett and his wife began serving at a poor peasant church when they were newly married. They immediately fell in love with the congregation. Seven years later, when they were called to pastor a bigger, more prosperous church, they packed up their wagons. But upon preparation to leave, they realized that they could not leave their dear people. Despite never receiving more than $200 a year, they continued their ministry at that little church for almost 55 years. King George III was especially fond of John's poetry. He offered to reward him with anything he wanted, but John refused, saying, "I have lived among my own people, enjoying their love. God has blessed my labors among them, and I need nothing which even a king could supply." John and his wife continued to live in meager conditions, but they could not be happier.

Matthew 6:33 says, "Seek first the kingdom of God and his righteousness, and all these things will be provided for you." God may call us to a ministry in life that makes little sense to the world. It may seem weird, unprofitable, unsuccessful, or even unimportant. Is God leading you to an opportunity that seems out of your league, fiscally irresponsible, or that will leave you isolated? God promises not to withhold any good thing (Psalm 84:11). He promises that if we put His work first, He will make sure we have everything we need. We work for His kingdom and not our own. In John's case, a lack in finances was a gain in friendships. If we submit in obedience to what God has asked of us, we will soon find that we will be the happiest people on the planet, no matter where we are.

Questions

In what ways does this hymn reflect the importance of Christian affection and brotherly love toward one another?

Meditate on Colossians 3:16. How does this verse encourage you to have a more abounding and abundant love to the believers around you?

What does this hymn, in light of Matthew 6:33, teach about working diligently unto the Lord?

God Leads His Dear Children Along

George A. Young, ca. 1903

In shady, green pastures, so rich and so sweet,
God leads His dear children along;
Where the water's cool flow bathes the weary one's feet,
God leads His dear children along.

Sometimes on the mount where the sun shines so bright,
God leads His dear children along;
Sometimes in the valley, in darkest of night,
God leads His dear children along.

Though sorrows befall us and Satan oppose,
God leads His dear children along;
Through grace we can conquer, defeat all our foes,
God leads His dear children along.

Away from the mire, and away from the clay,
God leads His dear children along;
Away up in glory, eternity's day,
God leads His dear children along.

Some through the waters, some through the flood,
Some through the fire, but all through the blood;
Some through great sorrow, but God gives a song,
In the night season and all the day long.

week 1
day 4

READ:
ISAIAH 43:1-2
PSALM 31:3
PSALM 61:1-2

God Leads His Dear Children Along

George A. Young was a devoted pastor in a rural area, often struggling to make ends meet. Despite a poor salary and very little to call their own, he and his wife served faithfully and without complaint. After much effort, they were finally able to scrape together the money to build a small house. They were ecstatic to finally have a place of their own to call home! Even though the Youngs were well-loved in their community, there were some people who did not appreciate their gospel message. One day, while the Youngs were in another area holding meetings, hoodlums came and burned their house to the ground, leaving nothing behind. It is said that after this devastating turn of events, George penned this beloved hymn declaring his continued devotion and loyalty to Jesus Christ and His sovereignty.

We often credit the Lord with the good things that happen in life. Let us not forget that He is always in control, during the good and the bad. Whether on the mountaintop, in a dark valley, in the middle of a battle, or in severe persecution, He has never left our side. In which season of life do you currently find yourself? If you are grazing on green pastures, thank God for this! If you find yourself looking at someone else's pasture, remember that an easy life is not the best thing we can have in this life. Jesus is all we need. Encourage your heart that He will not lead you to something without sustaining you through it. He is faithful in every season. Psalm 42:8 says it this way: "The Lord will send his faithful love by day; his song will be with me in the night—a prayer to the God of my life."

Questions

Read Psalm 61:1-2. What do you think the psalmist means by, "Lead me to the Rock that is high above me"? In what ways does this reflect the Lord and His character?

Meditate on Isaiah 43:1-2. In what ways does the hymn reflect this passage?

How does this hymn and the story behind it encourage you in your spiritual walk?

'Tis So Sweet To Trust in Jesus

Louisa M. R. Stead, ca. 1882

'Tis so sweet to trust in Jesus,
Just to take Him at His word;
Just to rest upon His promise,
And to know, "Thus saith the Lord!"

Oh, how sweet to trust in Jesus,
Just to trust His cleansing blood;
And in simple faith to plunge me
'Neath the healing, cleansing flood!

Yes, 'tis sweet to trust in Jesus,
Just from sin and self to cease;
Just from Jesus simply taking
Life and rest, and joy and peace.

I'm so glad I learned to trust Thee,
Precious Jesus, Savior, Friend;
And I know that Thou art with me,
Wilt be with me to the end.

Jesus, Jesus, how I trust Him!
How I've proved Him o'er and o'er;
Jesus, Jesus, precious Jesus!
Oh, for grace to trust Him more!

**week 1
day 5**

READ:

PROVERBS 3:5-6

PSALM 9:10

PSALM 20:7

'Tis so Sweet to Trust in Jesus

Louisa M. R. Stead was enjoying a picnic lunch with her husband and four-year-old daughter, Lily, next to the ocean one day when a boy swimming cried for help. He was caught in an undertow and was going under. Her husband immediately went to rescue him, but both of them drowned while Louisa and her daughter watched helplessly. While grieving, Louisa penned the words to this comforting hymn. Shortly thereafter, she and her daughter went to Africa to do mission work. Louisa served over two decades there before her death, but the people who she left behind were deeply moved by her legacy. Over 5,000 native Christians continued to sing this song in their native language.

There will be so many events in our lives that we cannot explain—tragedies that we wonder why God did not prevent. Orphans, widows, childless parents, disease. God does not promise to give us answers, but He does promise that He is in control. Psalm 9:10 says, "Those who know your name trust in you because you have not abandoned those who seek you, Lord." If we trust God when He tells us that He has forgiven us of our sin, how could we not trust Him with the details of our lives? What if we fully trusted Him with our cares, and as the song says, just from Jesus simply took life and rest, joy and peace? He offers this today—an exchange of our trust for His peace. We can take our Father at His Word, being confident that He keeps His promises.

Questions

Reflect on Proverbs 3:5-6. How does this passage provide comfort to you? Why is it important to lean fully on trusting God rather than yourself?

Read Psalm 9:10. How does this verse grow your understanding of knowing the Lord's name? Why might this be important?

What are some ways that this hymn points your heart and mind to worshiping God?

We can
trust Him with
the details
of our lives.

For you are
my rock and
my fortress;
you lead me
for your
name's sake.

PSALM 31:3

What are some of the ways that your understanding of God's character has been expanded throughout this week?

In what ways did studying these hymns teach you to worship the Lord more fully in all circumstances?

What was your favorite hymn to study this week? Why?

What passage of Scripture stood out to you the most this week? In what ways did it draw you nearer to God?

How can you practically apply what you have learned this week?

Choose a verse or passage from this week's reading to reflect on. How does this verse/passage point your relationship toward Christ?

In Christ There is No East or West

William Arthur Dunkerly, ca. 1908

In Christ there is no east or west,
in him no south or north,
but one great fellowship of love
throughout the whole wide earth.

In Christ shall true hearts everywhere
their high communion find.
His service is the golden cord
close-binding humankind.

Join hands, disciples of the faith,
whate'er your race may be.
All children of the living God
are surely kin to me.

In Christ now meet both east and west;
in him meet south and north.
All Christly souls are one in him
throughout the whole wide earth.

week 2
day 1

READ:

1 JOHN 4:20-21

GALATIANS 3:28

COLOSSIANS 3:13-14

In Christ There is No East or West

Although this hymn by William Arthur Dunkerley is not a popular one sung much today, there is a heart-warming story told about it all these years later. It is said that toward the end of World War II, there were two ships docked, waiting to be allowed back into their country. One ship was filled with Americans, and the other was filled with Japanese aliens. For 24 hours, they glared at each other from the rails of their ships. Suddenly, out of nowhere, someone began singing this hymn, and soon, all the soldiers joined in, singing in unison. Former enemies were now united under the banner of Jesus Christ.

We were all enemies of God before salvation. Romans 5:8 says, "But God proves his own love for us in that while we were still sinners, Christ died for us." What great love the Father has for us! He did not only die for His friends. He died for the people who hated Him. Who are we to choose who we will accept and who we will reject? Jesus asks this question: if we do not love one another, how could we love the Father whom we cannot see (1 John 4:20-21)? This is how we show that we are Jesus's disciples—by loving one another. Let us lay down our weapons and declare peace among God's people. Let us claim Galatians 5:13, which says, "For you were called to be free, brothers and sisters; only don't use this freedom as an opportunity for the flesh, bur serve one another through love."

Questions

How does this hymn reflect the ways that we should care and love for one another?

Meditate on Galatians 3:28. In what ways does the hymn reflect this truth?

Spend some time in self-examination after reading Colossians 3:13-14. Do the ways in which you express love for others reflect this passage?

Under His Wings

William Cushing, ca. 1896

Under His wings I am safely abiding
Tho' the night deepens and tempests are wild,
Still I can trust Him; I know He will keep me.
He has redeemed me, and I am His child.

Under His wings - what a refuge in sorrow!
How the heart yearningly turns to His rest!
Often when earth has no balm for my healing,
There I find comfort, and there I am blessed.

Under His wings, O what precious enjoyment!
There will I hide till life's trials are o'er;
Sheltered, protected, no evil can harm me,
Resting in Jesus, I'm safe evermore.

Under His wings, under His wings,
Who from His love can sever?
Under His wings my soul shall abide,
Safely abide forever.

week 2
day 2

READ:

PSALM 17:8

PSALM 57:1

PSALM 91:4

Under His Wings

William Cushing was a successful pastor for 27 years in several large churches. After his young wife passed away, he endured a period of deep depression. He developed a debilitating condition that caused him the loss of his speech. He was forced to step down from the pulpit at the age of 47. In despair and loneliness, he asked the Lord to give him a way to glorify Him despite his limited abilities. The Lord answered this prayer with the gift of hymn writing. William wrote hymns, several of which are well-known today, including "When He Cometh" (the Jewel Song) and "Hiding in Thee."

This is a wonderful example of how the Lord can make beautiful things out of tragedy if we are willing to be used by Him in what may be unorthodox ways. We may not understand God's plan or why He allows hard things in our lives, but we can be sure that He will make beauty from the ashes. Cushing is thought to have written over 300 gospel hymns, and his influence as a hymn writer far exceeded his successful years as a pastor. We may not feel like we have much to give, but the Lord can multiply it for His kingdom. God can do big things with some loaves and a couple of fish if we offer Him what we have.

This hymn's theme of a mother hen who tucks her chicks underneath her to keep them warm and safe is the same protection God offers us. Psalm 91:4 says, "He will cover you with his feathers; you will take refuge under his wings. His faithfulness will be a protective shield." There is refuge in the arms of our Savior—refuge from the world, the enemy, and our own evil desires. Let us run to Him.

Questions

In light of Psalm 17:8, how does this hymn encourage you to find comfort in closeness with God?

Read Psalm 57:1 and reflect. Do you seek to find refuge in the Lord?

How does the testimony of William Cushing give you hope despite dire and difficult circumstances?

Blessed Assurance

Fanny Crosby, ca. 1873

Blessed assurance, Jesus is mine!
Oh, what a foretaste of glory divine!
Heir of salvation, purchase of God,
Born of His Spirit, washed in His blood.

Perfect submission, perfect delight,
Visions of rapture now burst on my sight;
Angels, descending, bring from above
Echoes of mercy, whispers of love.

Perfect submission, all is at rest,
I in my Savior am happy and blest,
Watching and waiting, looking above,
Filled with His goodness, lost in His love.

This is my story, this is my song,
Praising my Savior all the day long;
This is my story, this is my song,
Praising my Savior all the day long.

week 2
day 3

READ:
ROMANS 8:38-39
JOHN 5:11-13
GALATIANS 4:7
PSALM 40:3

Blessed Assurance

Due to improper medical treatment when she was six weeks old, Fanny Crosby became blind. While many would have allowed bitterness to overtake them, Fanny used her disability as a way to encourage others. A man once pitied her for not being able to see. Fanny replied that if she had the choice, she would not desire to have her sight. She counted herself honored that when she got to heaven, the face of Jesus would be the first she would see. She writes with confidence, "I shall know Him by the prints of the nails in His Hand" ("My Savior First of All"). By reading her hymns, you would not know that this dear lady was blind. She speaks of Jesus hiding her soul in the cleft of the rock, "where rivers of pleasure I see" ("He Hideth My Soul").

Fanny Crosby is a beautiful example of a woman who could have basked in self-pity. What if we, like Fanny, decided not to let anything take away our joy in Christ? Her motto in life was, "O what a happy soul am I! Although I cannot see, I am resolved that in this world contented I will be." There will always be a multitude of excuses we can find to give for why we will not be effective doing the things God has called us to do. Perhaps Fanny will never know the gift that her 8,000 hymns gave to the world, because her focus was not on the world but her Savior. In another hymn, she writes, "Take the world, but give me Jesus, let me view His constant smile" ("Take the World, but Give Me Jesus"). May our lives reflect the words of our Lord spoken of Mary who anointed His feet with oil, the same words etched on Fanny's tombstone: "She hath done what she could."

Questions

In what ways does Fanny's life, in accordance with Romans 8:38-39, teach you about the power and security in loving God?

Reflect on Psalm 40:3. How does this verse encourage you to continually praise the Lord in all circumstances?

Meditate on the words of this hymn. What are some additional things that we have blessed assurance of in Christ?

Amazing Grace

John Newton, ca. 1779

Amazing grace! How sweet the sound
that saved a wretch like me!
I once was lost, but now am found;
Was blind, but now I see.

'Twas grace that taught my heart to fear,
And grace my fears relieved;
How precious did that grace appear
The hour I first believed!

Through many dangers, toils and snares,
I have already come;
'Tis grace hath brought me safe thus far,
And grace will lead me home.

The Lord has promised good to me,
His Word my hope secures;
He will my Shield and Portion be,
As long as life endures.

Yea, when this flesh and heart shall fail,
And mortal life shall cease,
I shall possess, within the veil,
A life of joy and peace.

The earth shall soon dissolve like snow,
The sun forbear to shine;
But God, Who called me here below,
Will be forever mine.

When we've been there ten thousand years,
Bright shining as the sun,
We've no less days to sing God's praise
Than when we'd first begun.

**week 2
day 4**

READ:

EPHESIANS 2:8-9

ROMANS 3:23-24

JOHN 1:14

Amazing Grace

At the age of eleven, John Newton left school to become a seaman and lead a despicable lifestyle. He eventually became involved in the slave-trade, capturing African natives and selling them into slavery. During a rather tumultuous storm, Newton became afraid for his life and found a copy of Thomas à Kempis's book The Imitation of Christ. While reading, he was miraculously converted.

Some years later, Newton became an ordained minister in Cambridge. Instead of the traditional psalms that were usually sung in services, he introduced some simple hymns to the worship time. When he saw the need for more hymns, he began to write some himself with the help of William Cowper. One such song was "Amazing Grace"—probably one of the best known hymns of all time. This man who was lost and blind had found Christ, and he would never be the same.

We all have things in our past that we are not proud to recall. Even Paul, who formerly persecuted and killed Christians, was able to put the past behind him in order to serve the Lord. We too have this responsibility and privilege. Paul gives this advice: "But one thing I do: forgetting what lies behind and reaching forward to what is ahead, I pursue as my goal the prize promised by God's heavenly call in Christ Jesus" (Philippians 3:13-14). We cannot allow the regrets of our past to detour us from obedience in the future. When we consider where Christ has brought us, we can proclaim with John Newton, "I remember two things: That I am a great sinner and that Christ is a great Savior!"

Questions

Read Ephesians 2:8-9. How does this passage enrich your understanding of the amazing grace spoken about in the hymn?

Spend some time reflecting on John 1:14. In what ways does this verse enhance your knowledge of God's character?

Spend some time in prayer, praising God for His grace and asking that He would continually renew and expand your understanding of the amazing grace that He offers.

It Is Well With My Soul

Horatio G. Spafford, ca. 1873

When peace like a river attendeth my way,
when sorrows like sea billows roll;
whatever my lot, thou hast taught me to say,
"It is well, it is well with my soul."

Though Satan should buffet, though trials should come,
let this blest assurance control:
that Christ has regarded my helpless estate,
and has shed his own blood for my soul.

My sin oh, the bliss of this glorious thought!
my sin, not in part, but the whole,
is nailed to the cross, and I bear it no more;
praise the Lord, praise the Lord, O my soul!

O Lord, haste the day when my faith shall be sight,
the clouds be rolled back as a scroll;
the trump shall resound and the Lord shall descend;
even so, it is well with my soul.

It is well with my soul;
it is well, it is well with my soul.

**week 2
day 5**

READ:

PSALM 46:1-3

JOHN 16:33

PSALM 29:11

It is Well With My Soul

After the Chicago fire of 1871, Horatio Spafford decided to take his family on a vacation to Europe to help Mr. Moody with his evangelistic meetings in Great Britain. He sent his wife and four daughters on ahead overseas, Horatio being detained in America for a short time. Halfway through the trip, their boat collided with another vessel and sank within twelve minutes. His four daughters drowned, leaving Horatio's wife as one of only a few survivors. Shortly thereafter, Horatio stood on the mast of the ship in deep despair as he headed to meet his grieving wife. As he passed through the waters where his daughters were said to have drowned, a sudden peace swept over him and filled his heart with such comfort that he immediately penned the words of this famous hymn.

This hymn is beautifully composed to include all the seasons of life in which we may find ourselves. Peace, loss and grief, trials, sin and redemption, and death. We are quick to give God praise for the times of blessing but often wonder where He is in our tragedy. The answer is that He is there, waiting for us to acknowledge His presence and lean into His strength and comfort. The glorious thought that consumed the author in the middle of his despair was that Christ had nailed all his sin to the cross. Colossians 2:14 says, "[God] erased the certificate of debt, with its obligations, that was against us and opposed to us, and has taken it away by nailing it to the cross." This alone gives us cause to glorify God, even when we may not understand the things He allows. When life does not make sense, let us cling to the cross that provides salvation that we will never be able to fathom.

Questions

Think about the imagery in Psalm 46:1-3. How does this passage, along with the background of the hymn, encourage your faith in God's peace to grow?

Meditate on John 16:33. What does this teach you about the peace of the Lord? How is the peace offered to us by God different from the peace that is offered by worldly things?

Spend some time in prayer, reciting Psalm 29:11 and asking that the Lord would continue to give you strength and peace as your relationship with Him grows.

Aknowledge
His presence and
lean into His
Strength & Comfort

Scripture Memory

For I am persuaded that neither death nor life, nor angels nor demons, nor things present nor things to come, nor powers, nor height nor depth, nor any other created thing will be able to separate us from the love of God that is in Christ Jesus our Lord.

ROMANS 8:38-39

Weekly Reflection

What are some of the ways that your understanding of God's character has been expanded throughout this week?

In what ways did studying these hymns teach you to worship the Lord more fully in all circumstances?

What was your favorite hymn to study this week? Why?

What passage of Scripture stood out to you the most this week? In what ways did it draw you nearer to God?

How can you practically apply what you have learned this week?

Choose a verse or passage from this week's reading to reflect on. How does this verse/passage point your relationship toward Christ?

I Will Sing of My Redeemer

Philip P. Bliss, ca. 1876

*I will sing of my Redeemer
and his wondrous love to me;
on the cruel cross he suffered,
from the curse to set me free.*

*I will tell the wondrous story,
how my lost estate to save,
in his boundless love and mercy,
he the ransom freely gave.*

*I will praise my dear Redeemer,
his triumphant power I'll tell:
how the victory he gives me over
sin and death and hell.*

*I will sing of my Redeemer
and his heavenly love for me;
he from death to life has brought me,
Son of God, with him to be.*

*Sing, O sing of my Redeemer!
With his blood he purchased me;
on the cross he sealed my pardon,
paid the debt, and made me free.*

**week 3
day 1**

READ:

ISAIAH 44:23-24

PSALM III:9

PSALM 107:2

I Will Sing of My Redeemer

Phillip P. Bliss concluded an evangelistic meeting in Chicago in 1876 with the words, "I may never pass this way again." On his trip home, the bridge under his train collapsed, and the back half of the train fell into the icy waters below. Bliss escaped, but upon realization that his wife was caught in the fire, he reentered the scene. Both of them burned in the flames, and neither of their bodies were ever found. Later, in one of the front train cars that made it over the bridge, they found Bliss's belongings. Inside, this newly written verse gives the idea that he knew his time was short.

This song is akin to the verse in Isaiah that says, "Rejoice, heavens, for the Lord has acted; shout, depths of the earth. Breakout into singing, mountains, forest, and every tree in it. For the Lord has redeemed Jacob, and glorifies himself through Israel. This is what the Lord, your Redeemer who formed you from the womb, says: I am the Lord who made everything" (Isaiah 44:23-24a).

Worship is not simply an act of praise for the present but a preparation for what is to come. We do not know the future, but by reading and meditating on God's Word, we can set our souls in a place of solace and peace for what is ahead. We are not guaranteed tomorrow, but we can be confident that our souls are always in the care of our loving Redeemer.

Questions

Read Isaiah 44:23-24. What do the similarities between this passage and the hymn express about the importance and richness of spending time in God's Word?

Look up the definition for the word "redeemer." How does this definition help you understand God's character as spoken about in the song?

Meditate on Psalm 107:2. What are some of the ways that the Lord has redeemed you from trouble?

Now Thank We All Our God

John Newton, ca. 1779

Now thank we all our God
with heart and hands and voices,
who wondrous things has done,
in whom his world rejoices;
who from our mothers' arms
has blessed us on our way
with countless gifts of love,
and still is ours today.

O may this bounteous God
through all our life be near us,
with ever joyful hearts
and blessed peace to cheer us,
to keep us in his grace,
and guide us when perplexed,
and free us from all ills
of this world in the next.

All praise and thanks to God
the Father now be given,
the Son and Spirit blest,
who reign in highest heaven
the one eternal God,
whom heaven and earth adore;
for thus it was, is now,
and shall be evermore.

week 3
day 2

READ:
I THESSALONIANS 5:18
COLOSSIANS 3:15
PSALM 107:1

Now Thank We All Our God

Martin Rinkart was the only ordained clergyman in the town of Eilenburg, Germany, during the Thirty Years' War. Being a walled city, the city was overcrowded with refugees and filled with disease. The bloodshed was devastating, and his wife also died during this time. Despite all he had been through and the lack of thankfulness on the part of the people he had helped, Martin did not let that prevent him from recognizing all of God's blessings.

What are you facing right now that seems bleak? What responsibilities have you been laden with that are thankless? What efforts are you putting forth behind the scenes that leave you weary and wondering if it is all worth it? Consider the ten lepers who came to Jesus for healing. Only one of them returned to express his appreciation to the Lord — a Samaritan. "Then Jesus said, 'Were not ten cleansed? Where are the nine? Didn't any return to give glory to God except this foreigner?'" (Luke 17:17-18). We too were once outsiders, enemies of the cross of Christ. But because of Jesus, we have been brought near. While this leper undoubtedly had lost his job, his social status, and possibly even his family, he chose to bypass the things that looked grim around him. He chose to focus on his healing and praise Jesus for it. We too can look around us and see poverty, loss, and tragedy; or, we can choose to see what Christ did for us. His forgiveness makes this life worth living. No matter how things look around us, there is always cause to praise Him.

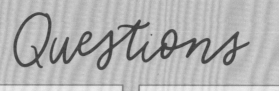

Questions

Reflect on 1 Thessalonians 5:18. How does this verse enrich your understanding of what it means to be thankful?

Read Colossians 3:15. How are peace and thankfulness related to one another?

Spend some time in prayer, reciting Psalm 107:1 and asking that God would grow your thankfulness toward Him.

Come Thou Fount of Every Blessing

Robert Robinson, ca. 1758

Come, thou Fount of every blessing,
tune my heart to sing thy grace;
streams of mercy, never ceasing,
call for songs of loudest praise.
Teach me some melodious sonnet,
sung by flaming tongues above.
Praise the mount I'm fixed upon it
mount of God's redeeming love.

Here I find my greatest treasure;
hither by thy help I've come;
and I hope, by thy good pleasure,
safely to arrive at home.
Jesus sought me when a stranger,
wandering from the fold of God;
he, to rescue me from danger,
bought me with his precious blood.

Oh, to grace how great a debtor
daily I'm constrained to be!
Let thy goodness, like a fetter,
bind my wandering heart to thee:
prone to wander, Lord, I feel it,
prone to leave the God I love;
here's my heart, O take and seal it;
seal it for thy courts above.

week 3
day 3

READ:
1 JOHN 4:19
PSALM 86:5
ROMANS 2:4

Come Thou Fount of Every Blessing

As a teenager, Robert Robinson ran in a gang and was labeled a hoodlum. He distinctly recalled going to a Methodist meeting held by George Whitefield with the intent and purpose of mocking the people and the message. Instead, God met with him there, and he was saved. He was shortly thereafter called to preach, and he wrote these words at just age 23: "Jesus sought me when a stranger, wandering from the fold of God; he, to rescue me from danger, bought me with his precious blood." Robert knew from personal experience whom Martin Luther called "The Hound of Heaven" pursuing his soul, calling him to repentance. In the last verse of the song, he referred to himself a debtor, recognizing the great sacrifice that Christ made on his behalf. Yet he goes on to say that he is a wanderer and asks for the handcuffs of grace to bind him to His Savior.

How is it possible to be a slave and a wanderer at the same time? We have freedom in Christ. We are not robots! God gives us a free will to come and go as we please. We too find ourselves in a place of wandering away from what we know is the Lord's best for us and seeking (what seem to be) greener pastures elsewhere. This goes back to Adam and Eve, set for life in the garden of Eden, yet seeking after the one thing to which they were not allowed access. How different our lives would be if we truly would bind ourselves to the Lord! The word "bind" means "to tie," but it also means "to cause to cohere in a single mass." May we be so bound to Christ that the world does not even see us—only Him.

Questions

Meditate on 1 John 4:19. In what ways does God's love compel you to love?

Read Psalm 86:5. In what ways does this psalm reflect the hymn?

Reflect on the second stanza. Do you find God to be your greatest treasure? What does it look like to treasure God?

Still, Still With Thee

Harriet B. Stowe, ca. 1853

Still, still with thee, when purple morning breaketh,
When the bird waketh, and the shadows flee;
Fairer than morning, lovelier than daylight,
Dawns the sweet consciousness, I am with thee.

Alone with thee, amid the mystic shadows,
The solemn hush of nature newly born;
Alone with thee in breathless adoration,
In the calm dew and freshness of the morn.

Still, still with thee, as to each newborn morning
A fresh and solemn splendor still is give,
So does this blessed consciousness, awakening,
Breathe each day nearness unto thee and heaven.

When sinks the soul, subdued by toil, to slumber,
Its closing eye looks up to thee in prayer;
Sweet the repose beneath thy wings overshading,
But sweeter still to wake and find thee there.

So shall it be at last, in that bright morning,
When the soul waketh and life's shadows flee;
O in that hour, fairer than daylight dawning,
Shall rise the glorious thought: I am with thee!

**week 3
day 4**

READ:

LUKE 10:38-42

JOSHUA 1:9

PSALM 73:23-28

Still, Still With Thee

Harriet Beecher Stowe was a writer who married a seminary professor, and together they had six children. Despite wearing many hats, she woke up at 4:30 each morning in order to "see the coming of the dawn, hear the singing of the birds, and to enjoy the overshadowing presence of her God." Toward the end of her life, she recalled that the one thread she could clearly see winding through her years as a busy mother involved in many pursuits was "the intense, unwavering sense of Christ's educating, guiding presence, and care."

How could Harriet fit in her writing career her passion for speaking out against slavery while being a devoted wife and mother? God gave her talents and zeal, and He also gave her the time necessary to do these things well. We can take some encouragement from a story in the Bible of two very different sisters—one, busy serving Jesus and the other, sitting at Jesus's feet. Hear the words that Jesus spoke to Martha's overwhelmed heart: "The Lord answered her, 'Martha, Martha, you are worried and upset about many things, but one thing is necessary. Mary has made the right choice, and it will not be taken away from her" (Luke 10:41-42.) We too have time to do what God has called us to do. Our callings are not meant to be burdens. Sometimes we can exaggerate our responsibilities and exhaust ourselves. But, if we keep the main things the main things and spend time with Jesus, He will make our priorities clear. We can wake up each day with a resolve to do just the things that we are called to do. Only then will we be able to impact the world by playing the role Christ has designed us to fill.

Questions

What does the story of Mary and Martha in Luke 10:38-42 teach you about our heart's posture toward the Lord? How is this reflected in the hymn?

What are some ways that you can set aside time to worship the Lord in similar ways to Harriet Beecher Stowe?

Meditate on Psalm 73:23-28. How does this passage grow your affection for God?

My Hope is Built on Nothing Less

Edward Mote, ca. 1834

My hope is built on nothing less
than Jesus' blood and righteousness;
I dare not trust the sweetest frame,
but wholly lean on Jesus' name.

When darkness veils his lovely face,
I rest on his unchanging grace;
in every high and stormy gale,
my anchor holds within the veil.

His oath, his covenant, his blood
support me in the whelming flood;
when all around my soul gives way,
he then is all my hope and stay.

When he shall come with trumpet sound,
O may I then in him be found,
dressed in his righteousness alone,
faultless to stand before the throne.

On Christ, the solid rock, I stand;
all other ground is sinking sand,
all other ground is sinking sand.

**week 3
day 5**

READ:

PSALM 31:1-3

PSALM 78:35

PSALM 62:7

My Hope is Built On Nothing Less

"I only want the pulpit, and when I cease to preach Christ, then turn me out of that." This was Edward Mote's response when he was offered a deed to church property. He served in that pulpit faithfully for many years but was forced to resign from ministry because of poor health one year before his death. He is noted as saying, "The truths I have been preaching, I am now living upon and they'll do very well to die upon." This song that he wrote years before would be ingrained in his memory in his dying moments.

The Bible often refers to Christ as the Rock. Even in the Old Testament, when Moses struck the rock and water came out, we see the imagery of God striking His Son, Jesus, to provide living water for us. Perhaps this passage was the inspiration for this song: "Therefore, everyone who hears these words of mine and acts on them will be like a wise man who built his house on the rock. The rain fell, the rivers rose, and the winds blew and pounded that house. Yet it didn't collapse, because its foundation was on the rock" (Matthew 7:24-25). If we find our identity in our financial status, body image, career, or children, won't our lives be a rollercoaster? With every shift in weight, promotion, lay off, performance, or behavior, we will lose our footing and crumble under the loss of the life we wanted to build. But with Jesus as our foundation, no storm will threaten our identity. Our circumstances do not change who God is, and likewise, our accomplishments or failures do not define who we are. Let us forsake the sand that tries to sink us and build on Christ, our solid Rock.

Questions

Read Psalm 62:7. Why might it be important to know that our salvation and help rests on God?

Reflect on Psalm 78:35. Why is it important to remember God as our rock?

Think about the descriptor of God as our rock. What are some ways you've experienced God as your rock?

Build on
Christ,
Our Solid
Rock.

Haven't I commanded you: be strong and courageous? Do not be afraid or discouraged, for the Lord your God is with you wherever you go.

JOSHUA 1:9

Weekly Reflection

What are some of the ways that your understanding of God's character has been expanded throughout this week?

In what ways did studying these hymns teach you to worship the Lord more fully in all circumstances?

What was your favorite hymn to study this week? Why?

What passage of Scripture stood out to you the most this week? In what ways did it draw you nearer to God?

How can you practically apply what you have learned this week?

Choose a verse or passage from this week's reading to reflect on. How does this verse/passage point your relationship toward Christ?

Take My Life and Let it Be

France R. Havergal, ca. 1874

Take my life and let it be
consecrated, Lord, to thee.
Take my moments and my days;
let them flow in endless praise,
let them flow in endless praise.

Take my hands and let them move
at the impulse of thy love.
Take my feet and let them be
swift and beautiful for thee,
swift and beautiful for thee.

Take my voice and let me sing
always, only, for my King
Take my lips and let them be
filled with messages from thee,
filled with messages from thee.

Take my silver and my gold;
not a mite would I withhold.
Take my intellect and use
every power as thou shalt choose,
every power as thou shalt choose.

Take my will and make it thine;
it shall be no longer mine.
Take my heart it is thine own;
it shall be thy royal throne,
it shall be thy royal throne.

Take my love; my Lord, I pour
at thy feet its treasure store.
Take myself, and I will be
ever, only, all for thee,
ever, only, all for thee.

**week 4
day 1**

READ:
ROMANS 12:1
GALATIANS 2:20
JOHN 15:1-7

Take My Life And Let it Be

Frances Havergal is known to this day as "the consecration poet." Her dedication to committing her life completely to the Lord is demonstrated particularly in two lines of this meaningful song. When she wrote, "Take my silver and my gold," she had in mind the instance when she sent about fifty pieces of heirloom and costly jewelry to the church to be used in evangelistic work. She was thrilled to offer these things to benefit the kingdom. Also the line, "Take my voice and let me sing only, always for my King," is a reference to personal sacrifice. Frances had an amazingly talented voice and could have been famous using her gift to entertain others. Instead, she chose to lead a quiet life, using her voice only in worship to God.

Romans 12:1 says, "Therefore, brothers and sisters, in view of the mercies of God, I urge you to present your bodies as a living sacrifice, holy and pleasing to God; this is your true worship." We may look at our lives and think we have given Him everything we can, but He has a way of seeping into the crevices and finding areas that are still hidden from His control. Any area that we hold back from God is an area of disobedience. Are we offering our lives as a living sacrifice? Are there areas that He has been pressing on, seeking our surrender? Are we giving Him just the parts we want to, or are we giving all of our lives, as a holy, acceptable sacrifice? Just as Christ held nothing back from us, may we follow His example, joyfully giving Him our all.

Questions

Look up the word "consecrated." How does this definition help you understand the hymn?

Meditate on Galatians 2:20. What does it mean to be crucified with Christ?

In light of John 15:1-7, what are some practical ways you can abide in Christ?

Jesus Loves Me

Anna B. Warner, ca. 1859

Jesus loves me, this I know,
for the Bible tells me so.
Little ones to Him belong;
they are weak, but He is strong

Jesus loves me he who died
heaven's gate to open wide.
He will wash away my sin,
let his little child come in.

Jesus loves me, this I know,
as he loved so long ago,
taking children on his knee,
saying, "Let them come to me."

Yes, Jesus loves me!
Yes, Jesus loves me!
Yes, Jesus loves me!
The Bible tells me so.

week 4
day 2

READ:

JOHN 3:16

1 JOHN 3:1

1 JOHN 4:10

Jesus Loves Me

Anna Bartlett Warner wrote several poems that were put to music, many of them specifically for children. The most famous text put to music she left behind is "Jesus Loves Me." While we may not know much about Anna, we know her confidence in the love of Jesus was enough to get her through any circumstance in life. Although we think of this as a children's song, it applies to us no matter what our age. The Bible often refers to us as children. 1 John 3:1 says, "See what great love the Father has given us that we should be called God's children—and we are!" In fact, child-like faith is required to enter heaven. Matthew 18:3 says, "'Truly I tell you,' he said, 'unless you turn and become like children, you will never enter the kingdom of heaven.'"

From our earliest memories, we dream of being a grown-up. We want to do things ourselves. We are eager to take responsibility, manage our freedom, and have a job. Then, once we have those things, we realize how messy these things are. Being an adult is not as fun as it would seem at times. Life is riddled with frustrations, worries, exhaustion, and a lot of hard work. Sometimes we just need to go back to the basics. We can get so caught up in theological debates, questions about life, and balancing grief and joy that we can forget the simplest of truths. Jesus loves us. He is for us. His Word is for us. If your heart is heavy today, go back to this simple truth you learned in Sunday school—Jesus loves me, this I know!

Questions

Think about the last line of the hymn. Why is it important to know what the Bible says about God's love for us?

In what ways is 1 John 4:10 reflected in this hymn?

Meditate on 1 John 3:1. In light of this verse and the hymn, why is it important to see ourselves as God's children?

Holy Bible,
Book Divine

John Burton, ca. 1803

Holy Bible, Book divine,
Precious treasure, thou art mine:
Mine to tell me whence I came;
Mine to teach me what I am.

Mine to chide me when I rove,
Mine to show a Savior's love;
Mine thou art to guide and guard;
Mine to punish or reward.

Mine to comfort in distress,
Suffering in this wilderness;
Mine to show by living faith,
We can triumph over death.

Mine to tell of joys to come,
And the rebel sinner's doom:
O thou holy book divine,
Precious treasure thou art mine.

**week 4
day 3**

READ:

2 TIMOTHY 3:16-17

HEBREWS 4:12

PSALM 19:7-11

*Holy Bible,
Book Divine*

John Burton, Sr. taught Sunday school because he had a passion to teach young children spiritual truths. This is one song that he wrote with the intent to teach children the importance of the Scriptures. The Bible is not a book about us. It is a book about God. John 5:39-40 says, "Your pore over the Scriptures because you think you have eternal life in them, and yet they testify about me. But you are not willing to come to me so that you may have life." May we not view the Bible as simply a way to get eternal life but as a way to draw closer to Jesus. When we read it to learn who God is, we will love Him more, desire to serve Him better, and feel conviction when we pursue lesser things.

Christians in other countries who are persecuted for their faith cling to God's Word like a child to its mother. If they can find any small scrap of paper, they will write down Bible verses that they can recall from memory. They risk the beatings they have been threatened with if they are found with Scripture. But it is so precious to them that they are willing to face any punishment just to have it near them. This is convicting to someone who has multiple Bibles sitting around the house, some never used. Do we see the Bible just as a tool? As a book we need to read? Or as a beautiful mirror that will make our hearts more lovely as we look into it? God's Word is a gift to be adored, cherished, and treasured. The more we see Christ on the pages of His Word, the more we will obey it, respect it, and love it.

Questions

Read 2 Timothy 3:16-17. How is this passage reflected in the words of the hymn?

Why is it important to have a proper understanding of God's Word?

Reflect on Hebrews 4:12. What does it mean that the Word of God is living and active?

How Great Thou Art

Carl Gustav Boberg, ca. 1885

Oh Lord my God
When I in awesome wonder
Consider all the worlds
Thy hands have made
I see the stars
I hear the rolling thunder
Thy power throughout
The universe displayed

And when I think of God,
His Son not sparing,
Sent Him to die,
I scarce can take it in;
That on the cross, my burden
gladly bearing He bled and died
to take away my sin

When Christ shall come
With shout of acclamation
And take me home
What joy shall fill my heart
Then I shall bow
With humble adoration
And then proclaim My God
How great Thou art

Then sings my soul
My Savior, God, to Thee
How great Thou art
How great Thou art

Then sings my soul
My Savior, God, to Thee
How great Thou art
How great Thou art

week 4
day 4

READ:

DEUTERONOMY 3:24

JEREMIAH 10:6

PSALM 96:4

How Great Thou Art

The author of this song, Carl Gustav Boberg, was suddenly caught in a terrifying thunderstorm, complete with lightning and thunder. As quickly as it began, it ended, and the blue skies rolled in with birds chirping and the sun shining. He fell to his knees in praise and composed this song. Oh, that we could experience moments where we sense anew the greatness and beauty of the Lord! It would change how we live. It would change our attitude toward life. Moses understood how high and mighty the Lord was. He says this in Deuteronomy 3:24: "Lord God, you have begun to show your greatness and your strong hand to your servant, for what god is there in heaven or on earth who can perform deeds and mighty acts like yours?"

In our culture, the word "great" is overused. We say that God is great. And so is our pizza.

But God is so much greater than anything we have felt here on the earth. Have you recently experienced His magnitude? Have you taken time to praise Him for His incredible work of creation and the ongoing work that He does in our hearts? Just one look at creation tells us that the same God who designed the intricate details of plants, animals, and people is fully capable of handling the minute details of our lives. Take a few minutes today to sit and wonder, to bathe in His glory and be in awe of Him. Let us consider the immensity of our sin and the sacrifice of His Son that carried our burden instead of us. Let us prepare for when Christ will take us to be with Him, and we will see Him face to face. And let us allow that future joy to penetrate our hearts even now as we anticipate His coming and His presence with us today.

Questions

Meditate on Deuteronomy 3:24. How does this verse aid you in understanding the greatness of God?

Reflect on Jeremiah 10:6. What are some of the ways you have seen God's greatness displayed in your life?

Spend some time in self-examination. Do you find yourself praising God for His greatness often? What are some ways that this hymn helps you to do so?

All Scripture is inspired by God and is profitable for teaching, rebuking, for correcting, for training in righteousness, so that the man of God may be complete, equipped for every good work.

2 TIMOTHY 3:16-17

Weekly Reflection

What are some of the ways that your understanding of God's character has been expanded throughout this week?

In what ways did studying these hymns teach you to worship the Lord more fully in all circumstances?

What was your favorite hymn to study this week? Why?

What passage of Scripture stood out to you the most this week? In what ways did it draw you nearer to God?

How can you practically apply what you have learned this week?

Choose a verse or passage from this week's reading to reflect on. How does this verse/passage point your relationship toward Christ?

What is the Gospel?

THANK YOU FOR READING AND ENJOYING THIS STUDY WITH US! WE ARE ABUNDANTLY GRATEFUL FOR THE WORD OF GOD, THE INSTRUCTION WE GLEAN FROM IT, AND THE EVER-GROWING UNDERSTANDING IT PROVIDES FOR US OF GOD'S CHARACTER. WE ARE ALSO THANKFUL THAT SCRIPTURE CONTINUALLY POINTS TO ONE THING IN INNUMERABLE WAYS: THE GOSPEL.

We remember our brokenness when we read about the fall of Adam and Eve in the garden of Eden (Genesis 3), where sin entered into a perfect world and maimed it. We remember the necessity that something innocent must die to pay for our sin when we read about the atoning sacrifices in the Old Testament. We read that we have all sinned and fallen short of the glory of God (Romans 3:23) and that the penalty for our brokenness, the wages of our sin, is death (Romans 6:23). We all need grace and mercy, but most importantly, we all need a Savior.

We consider the goodness of God when we realize that He did not plan to leave us in this dire state. We see His promise to buy us back from the clutches of sin and death in Genesis 3:15. And we see that promise accomplished with Jesus Christ on the cross. Jesus Christ knew no sin yet became sin so that we might become righteous through His sacrifice (2 Corinthians 5:21). Jesus was tempted in every way that we are and lived sinlessly. He was reviled yet still yielded Himself for our sake, that we may have life abundant in Him. Jesus lived the perfect life that we could not live and died the death that we deserved.

The gospel is profound yet simple. There are many mysteries in it that we will never understand this side of heaven, but there is still overwhelming weight to its implications in this life. The gospel tells of our sinfulness and God's goodness and a gracious gift that compels a response. We are saved by grace through faith, which means that we rest with faith in the grace that Jesus Christ displayed on the cross (Ephesians 2:8-9). We cannot save ourselves from our brokenness or do any amount of good works to merit God's favor. Still, we can have faith that what Jesus accomplished in His death, burial, and resurrection was more than enough for our salvation and our eternal delight. When we accept God, we are commanded to die to ourselves and our sinful desires and live a life worthy of the calling we have received (Ephesians 4:1). The gospel compels us to be sanctified, and in so doing, we are conformed to the likeness of Christ Himself. This is hope. This is redemption. This is the gospel.

SCRIPTURES TO REFERENCE:

GENESIS 3:15

I will put hostility between you and the woman, and between your offspring and her offspring. He will strike your head, and you will strike his heel.

ROMANS 3:23

For all have sinned and fall short of the glory of God.

ROMANS 6:23

For the wages of sin is death, but the gift of God is eternal life in Christ Jesus our Lord.

2 CORINTHIANS 5:21

He made the one who did not know sin to be sin for us, so that in him we might become the righteousness of God.

EPHESIANS 2:8-9

For you are saved by grace through faith, and this is not from yourselves; it is God's gift — not from works, so that no one can boast.

EPHESIANS 4:1-3

Therefore I, the prisoner in the Lord, urge you to walk worthy of the calling you have received, with all humility and gentleness, with patience, bearing with one another in love, making every effort to keep the unity of the Spirit through the bond of peace.

Thank You

for studying God's Word with us

CONNECT WITH US

@THEDAILYGRACECO
@DAILYGRACEPODCAST

CONTACT US

INFO@THEDAILYGRACECO.COM

SHARE

#THEDAILYGRACECO

VISIT US ONLINE

THEDAILYGRACECO.COM

MORE DAILY GRACE!

THE DAILY GRACE APP
DAILY GRACE PODCAST